Astro
Cat

Maverick
Early Readers

'Astro Cat'
An original concept by Clare Helen Welsh
© Clare Helen Welsh

Illustrated by Junissa Bianda

Published by MAVERICK ARTS PUBLISHING LTD
Studio 11, City Business Centre, 6 Brighton Road,
Horsham, West Sussex, RH13 5BB
© Maverick Arts Publishing Limited August 2020
+44 (0)1403 256941

A CIP catalogue record for this book is available at the British Library.

ISBN 978-1-84886-679-9

www.maverickbooks.co.uk

Blue

This book is rated as: Blue Band (Guided Reading)
This story is mostly decodable at Letters and Sounds Phase 4.
Up to five non-decodable story words are included.

Astro
Cat

by **Clare Helen Welsh**
illustrated by **Junissa Bianda**

Star is Ella's pet cat.

When Ella is out, Star turns into...

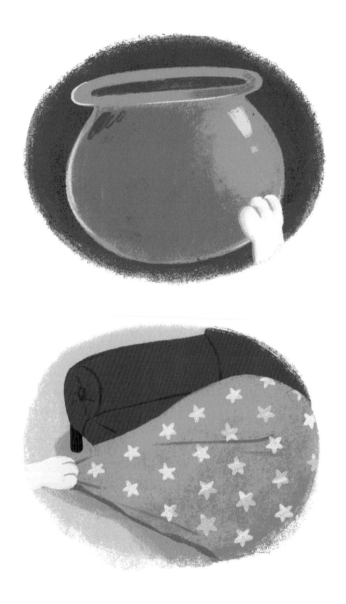

...Astro Cat!

Astro Cat has a helmet and cloak.

Astro Cat sees something.

Bump! Bump!

It's a monster with lots of fur!

Astro Cat jumps on it.

Then Astro Cat sees Pip

stuck in the milk.

What will she do?

Astro Cat pulls Pip out
with her long tail.

Then something jumps out of
a black hole. Swish! Swoosh!

It's Turbo Tom! He has a light gun.

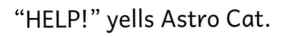

"HELP!" yells Astro Cat.

But no help comes.

What will she do?

Something creeps up Turbo Tom's leg...

...then runs down his long tail.

Pip nips Turbo Tom!

Astro Cat grabs the light gun!

Turbo Tom runs off as fast as he can!

But then Astro Cat hears something.

Click! Click!

Astro Cat needs to get back,

or Ella might see she is missing.

Quiz

1. Star is _____'s pet cat.
a) Bill
b) Ella
c) Tom

2. What does Astro Cat wear?
a) A box and lid
b) A hat and cloth
c) A helmet and cloak

3. Who jumps through the black hole?
a) Turbo Tom
b) Pip
c) Rocket Ron

4. Who helps Astro Cat?

a) Pip

b) Ella

c) Turbo Tom

5. What does Astro Cat hear?

a) Knock! Knock!

b) Run! Run!

c) Click! Click!

Turn over for answers

Book Bands for Guided Reading

The Institute of Education book banding system is a scale of colours that reflects the various levels of reading difficulty. The bands are assigned by taking into account the content, the language style, the layout and phonics. Word, phrase and sentence level work is also taken into consideration.

Maverick Early Readers are a bright, attractive range of books covering the pink to white bands. All of these books have been book banded for guided reading to the industry standard and edited by a leading educational consultant.

Pink
Red
Yellow
Blue
Green
Orange
Turquoise
Purple
Gold
White

To view the whole Maverick Readers scheme, visit our website at
www.maverickearlyreaders.com

Or scan the QR code above to view our scheme instantly!

Quiz Answers: 1b, 2c, 3a, 4a, 5c